3–5

Homework Pages
for Independent Reading

75 High-Interest Reproducibles That Guide Kids to Apply Reading Strategies, Explore Genre and Literary Elements, and Expand Vocabulary With Any Book

Pam Allyn & Georgie Marley

SCHOLASTIC

New York • Toronto • London • Auckland • Sydney
Mexico City • New Delhi • Hong Kong • Buenos Aires

Dedication

For my daughters, Katie and Charlotte,
who teach me that anything fun always gets done.

—Pam

For my children, Jess and Ben, for reminding me that
each day is an opportunity for new journeys of discovery.

—Georgie

Acknowledgments

With appreciation for Joanna Davis-Swing and Sarah Glasscock,
brilliant editors who take good care of ideas.

A special thanks to the entire Scholastic team for championing
the reading lives of children.

Cover design: Jorge J. Namerow
Cover photograph: Media Bakery
Interior design: Sarah Morrow
Interior illustrations: Steve Cox (pp. 37, 59, 65, 70, 71)
Other illustrations: Teresa Anderko, Maxie Chambliss, and Dave Clegg
Development Editor: Joanna Davis-Swing
Editor: Sarah Glasscock

ISBN: 978-0-545-38542-8

Contents

Introduction

Our aim in this book is to create the kind of homework that students will really want to do, the kind of homework that both supplements and enhances their work in school, the kind of homework that the entire family can learn from and that brings the work of school and home closer together. These homework activities have been designed to cultivate lifelong skills and a love for reading in students.

Students must practice both inside of and outside of school to build good reading habits. As each student in your class is probably reading at varying levels of text complexity, these activities give you, your students, and their families a structured approach to building reading skills during independent reading.

What Is Independent Reading?

Independent reading is the crucial practice readers do on their own, but not necessarily completely by themselves, as they incorporate the expert guidance that a teacher has provided. All children must be given the opportunity every day to practice their emerging readership skills. Independent reading means that children are making choices about what to read and are engaged directly with a text; they are given time to absorb and understand it in their own way. But for the growing child, independent reading requires the supervision and involvement of the teacher and family members. Simply put: to become a proficient reader, one needs the opportunity to read. Students learn how to become proficient readers by participating in independent reading in the classroom and then practicing those skills at home.

Developing readers should read independently for increasing periods of time to build their stamina both in school and at home. The research of educators including Allington (2012) and Hiebert and Reutzel (2010) has helped us arrive at the following formula for determining how much time a child should spend on independent reading: multiply the child's grade level by 10 minutes (e.g., third grade: 3 x 10 = 30 minutes). For a child who excels or one who struggles, adjust the formula up or down.

The Importance of Independent Reading

Richard Allington found a direct correlation between the amount of time spent reading and reading performance (2012). Allington emphasizes that in order for children to progress as readers, they need to practice reading to build volume, stamina, and fluency. The amount of time students spend reading independently is the best predictor of reading achievement.

Many students struggle with reading or dislike reading because they find the texts assigned in school to be uninteresting, unchallenging, or too difficult to read. When students choose their own texts for independent reading, they are more motivated to practice the reading skills we teach them in and out of the classroom. The activities in this book will enhance their reading experience and give you a way to monitor their independent reading progress.

How to Use This Book

Just as we want our students to choose their own texts for independent reading, we also want you to choose which activities your students will work on independently at home. You can use the activities in this book in many different ways. Here are some suggestions:

- After you have taught a skill or a related skill in class, consult the contents to find activities that address it. Have all of your students complete the same activity using their own independent reading text.

- After meeting with a group, assign a specific activity to those students for independent follow-up. You may have different groups practicing different skills based on the work you have done with them.

- After working on a specific skill with an individual student, assign an activity that addresses that skill. You may also take this approach to differentiate homework for students who need additional support in developing a particular skill.

- Let students choose an activity from a variety of the homework activities that you have selected. A recent study found that students who were allowed to choose their own homework assignment from a number of acceptable options reported higher intrinsic motivation, felt more competent, and performed better on unit assessments than those who were assigned specific homework (Patall, Cooper, & Wynn, 2010).

Some of the activities may be used on a daily basis while others require students to complete texts before using them. For the latter situation, consider giving the activity to students on Monday and asking them to return the completed page later in the week.

Common Core State Standards for Reading

The activities in this book correlate to the Common Core State Standards (CCSS) formally adopted by most states. We explain below the correlations of the activities to the key areas of the CCSS College and Career Readiness Anchor Standards for Reading. The specific Reading Standards for Literature and for Informational Text for Grades 3–5 follow on pages 8–11. Each activity is correlated to these standards on the overview page for each section.

Key Ideas and Details ⌐

1 Read closely to determine what the text says explicitly and to make logical inferences from it; cite specific textual evidence when writing or speaking to support conclusions drawn from the text.

2 Determine central ideas or themes of a text and analyze their development; summarize the key supporting details and ideas.

3 Analyze how and why individuals, events, and ideas develop and interact over the course of a text.

Strong readers are good at analyzing as they read. To help our students become strong readers, we ask them to show their understanding of a text by using evidence from the text to support their thinking. The activities in the "Literary Elements" and "Reading Responses" sections ask students to reflect on their reading of a variety of text types and to analyze them.

Craft and Structure ⌐

4 Interpret words and phrases as they are used in a text, including determining technical, connotative, and figurative meanings, and analyze how specific word choices shape meaning or tone.

5 Analyze the structure of texts, including how specific sentences, paragraphs, and larger portions of the text (e.g., a section, chapter, scene, or stanza) relate to each other and the whole.

6 Assess how point of view or purpose shapes the content and style of a text.

Students must be able to analyze the effects of a text's structure on the author's overall message. This is one of many tools that will help them understand the purpose of the text. The "Language" section asks students to analyze texts, including specific sentences and vocabulary, to show their understanding of text structures and how (and why) authors craft their texts.

Integration of Knowledge and Ideas ⌐

7 Integrate and evaluate content presented in diverse media and formats, including visually and quantitatively, as well as in words.

8 Delineate and evaluate the argument and specific claims in a text, including the validity of the reasoning as well as the relevance and sufficiency of the evidence.

9 Analyze how two or more texts address similar themes or topics in order to build knowledge or to compare the approaches the authors take.

The CCSS ask students to read from a wide and deep selection of literary and informational texts. After reading, they are often asked to apply their newfound knowledge. The activities in the "Reading Response" section encourage students to apply their new knowledge in a variety of engaging ways. We ask them to comprehend and critique literary texts using higher-level thinking skills that demonstrate their knowledge. In the activities in the "Informational Text" section, students build strong content knowledge in preparation for composing informational text. They must use text features and structure with purpose to access information efficiently and effectively.

Range of Reading and Level of Text Complexity ⌐

10 Read and comprehend complex literary and informational texts independently and proficiently.

The CCSS state that students "should acquire the habits of reading independently and closely, which are essential to their future success." The activities in this book ensure that the following college and career ready standards are being addressed in the classroom and practiced at home.

CCSS Reading Standards for Literature

GRADE 3	GRADE 4	GRADE 5
Key Ideas and Details —		
1. Ask and answer questions to demonstrate understanding of a text, referring explicitly to the text as the basis for the answers.	**1.** Refer to details and examples in a text when explaining what the text says explicitly and when drawing inferences from the text.	**1.** Quote accurately from a text when explaining what the text says explicitly and when drawing inferences from the text.
2. Recount stories, including fables, folktales, and myths from diverse cultures; determine the central message, or moral, and explain how it is conveyed through key details in the text.	**2.** Determine a theme of a story, drama, or poem from details in the text; summarize the text.	**2.** Determine a theme of a story, drama, or poem from details in the text, including how characters in a story or drama respond to challenges or how the speaker in a poem reflects upon a topic; summarize the text.
3. Describe characters in a story (e.g., their traits, motivations, or feelings) and explain how their actions contribute to the sequence of events.	**3.** Describe in depth a character, setting, or event in a story or drama, drawing on specific details in the text (e.g., a character's thoughts, words, or actions).	**3.** Compare and contrast two or more characters, settings, or events in a story or drama, drawing on specific details in the text (e.g., how characters interact).
Craft and Structure —		
4. Determine the meaning of words and phrases as they are used in a text, distinguishing literal from nonliteral language.	**4.** Determine the meaning of words and phrases as they are used in a text, including those that allude to significant characters found in mythology (e.g., *Herculean*).	**4.** Determine the meaning of words and phrases as they are used in a text, including figurative language such as metaphors and similes.
5. Refer to parts of stories, dramas, and poems when writing or speaking about a text, using terms such as chapter, scene, and stanza; describe how each successive part builds on earlier sections.	**5.** Explain major differences between poems, drama, and prose, and refer to the structural elements of poems (e.g., verse, rhythm, meter) and drama (e.g., casts of characters, settings, descriptions, dialogue, stage directions) when writing or speaking about a text.	**5.** Explain how a series of chapters, scenes, or stanzas fit together to provide the overall structure of a particular story, drama, or poem.
6. Distinguish their own point of view from that of the narrator or those of the characters.	**6.** Compare and contrast the point of view from which different stories are narrated, including the difference between first- and third-person narrations.	**6.** Describe how a narrator's or speaker's point of view influences how events are described.

GRADE 3	GRADE 4	GRADE 5
Integration of Knowledge and Ideas —		
7. Explain how specific aspects of a text's illustrations contribute to what is conveyed by the words in a story (e.g., create mood, emphasize aspects of a character or setting).	**7.** Make connections between the text of a story or drama and a visual or oral presentation of the text, identifying where each version reflects specific descriptions and directions in the text.	**7.** Analyze how visual and multimedia elements contribute to the meaning, tone, or beauty of a text (e.g., graphic novel, multimedia presentation of fiction, folktale, myth, poem).
8. (Not applicable to literature)	**8.** (Not applicable to literature)	**8.** (Not applicable to literature)
9. Compare and contrast the themes, settings, and plots of stories written by the same author about the same or similar characters (e.g., in books from a series).	**9.** Compare and contrast the treatment of similar themes and topics (e.g., opposition of good and evil) and patterns of events (e.g., the quest) in stories, myths, and traditional literature from different cultures.	**9.** Compare and contrast stories in the same genre (e.g., mysteries and adventure stories) on their approaches to similar themes and topics.
Range of Reading and Level of Text Complexity —		
10. By the end of the year, read and comprehend literature, including stories, dramas, and poetry, at the high end of the grades 2–3 complexity band independently and proficiently.	**10.** By the end of the year, read and comprehend literature, including stories, dramas, and poetry, at the high end of the grades 4–5 complexity band proficiently, with scaffolding as needed at the high end of the range.	**10.** By the end of the year, read and comprehend literature, including stories, dramas, and poetry, at the high end of the grades 4–5 complexity band independently and proficiently.

CCSS Reading Standards for Informational Literature

GRADE 3	GRADE 4	GRADE 5
Key Ideas and Details —		
1. Ask and answer questions to demonstrate understanding of a text, referring explicitly to the text as the basis for the answers.	**1.** Refer to details and examples in a text when explaining what the text says explicitly and when drawing inferences from the text.	**1.** Quote accurately from a text when explaining what the text says explicitly and when drawing inferences from the text.
2. Determine the main idea of a text; recount the key details and explain how they support the main idea.	**2.** Determine the main idea of a text and how it is supported by key details; summarize the text.	**2.** Determine two or more main ideas of a text and explain how they are supported by key details; summarize the text.

GRADE 3	GRADE 4	GRADE 5
3. Describe the relationship between a series of historical events, scientific ideas or concepts, or steps in technical procedures in a text, using language that pertains to time, sequence, and cause/effect.	**3.** Explain events, procedures, ideas, or concepts in a historical, scientific, or technical text, including what happened and why, based on specific information in the text.	**3.** Explain the relationships or interactions between two or more individuals, events, ideas, or concepts in a historical, scientific, or technical text based on specific information in the text.

Craft and Structure –

GRADE 3	GRADE 4	GRADE 5
4. Determine the meaning of general academic and domain-specific words and phrases in a text relevant to a grade 3 topic or subject area.	**4.** Determine the meaning of general academic and domain-specific words and phrases in a text relevant to a grade 4 topic or subject area.	**4.** Determine the meaning of general academic and domain-specific words and phrases in a text relevant to a grade 5 topic or subject area.
5. Use text features and search tools (e.g., key words, sidebars, hyperlinks) to locate information relevant to a given topic efficiently.	**5.** Describe the overall structure (e.g., chronology, comparison, cause/effect, problem/solution) of events, ideas, concepts, or information in a text or part of a text.	**5.** Compare and contrast the overall structure (e.g., chronology, comparison, cause/effect, problem/solution) of events, ideas, concepts, or information in two or more texts.
6. Distinguish their own point of view from that of the author of a text.	**6.** Compare and contrast a first-hand and secondhand account of the same event or topic; describe the differences in focus and the information provided.	**6.** Analyze multiple accounts of the same event or topic, noting important similarities and differences in the point of view they represent.

Integration of Knowledge and Ideas –

GRADE 3	GRADE 4	GRADE 5
7. Use information gained from illustrations (e.g., maps, photographs) and the words in a text to demonstrate understanding of the text (e.g., where, when, why, and how key events occur).	**7.** Interpret information presented visually, orally, or quantitatively (e.g., in charts, graphs, diagrams, time lines, animations, or interactive elements on Web pages) and explain how the information contributes to an understanding of the text in which it appears.	**7.** Draw on information from multiple print or digital sources, demonstrating the ability to locate an answer to a question quickly or to solve a problem efficiently.
8. Describe the logical connection between particular sentences and paragraphs in a text (e.g., comparison, cause/effect, first/second/third in a sequence.)	**8.** Explain how an author uses reasons and evidence to support particular points in a text.	**8.** Explain how an author uses reasons and evidence to support particular points in a text, identifying which reasons and evidence support which point(s).

GRADE 3	GRADE 4	GRADE 5
9. Compare and contrast the most important points and key details presented in two texts on the same topic.	**9.** Integrate information from two texts on the same topic in order to write or speak about the subject knowledgeably.	**9.** Integrate information from several texts on the same topic in order to write or speak about the subject knowledgeably.
Range of Reading and Level of Text Complexity —		
10. By the end of the year, read and comprehend informational texts, including history/social studies, science, and technical texts, at the high end of the grades 2–3 text complexity band independently and proficiently.	**10.** By the end of the year, read and comprehend informational texts, including history/social studies, science, and technical texts, in the grades 4–5 text complexity band proficiently, with scaffolding as needed at the high end of the range.	**10.** By the end of the year, read and comprehend informational texts, including history/social studies, science, and technical texts, at the high end of the grades 4–5 text complexity band independently and proficiently.

Leveled Text Appendix

When you provide a rich variety of texts, you are communicating to students that reading is a worthwhile and valuable activity and setting the stage for them to develop good, lifelong reading habits. Ensuring that students have access to a wide range of materials is imperative when offering independent practice. Students should have easy access to a variety of reading materials from an array of genres and text types including magazines, real-life documents, resource materials, and Internet resources. The appendix contains titles of some of our favorite independent reading texts at a variety of levels that students can read at home. There are, of course, thousands of titles; these are just a select few as a sampling.

Conclusion

Independence is the key outcome for the Common Core State Standards and for all we do as teachers and education leaders. We want our students to leave our classrooms and enter into the world fully engaged with texts in ways that can change their lives. The work our students do between home and school is a crucial bridge to building their strengths as lifelong readers. Let this book and the resources inside it be a valuable tool to build that bridge, so we can fortify independence in all children and open them up to the world of reading, now and always.

Independence and Stamina: Overview

One of the key goals of the Common Core State Standards is for students to demonstrate reading independence. The activities in this section address a main concern of many teachers: How do I know my students are reading at home and becoming self-directed learners? Assessing students' work on the reproducibles allows you to see what they are reading, how long they are reading, and whether they are meeting their personal reading goals. In this section, students record their reading; they are also asked to reflect on their reading, to think about genre, and to form an opinion of the text—and they accomplish all of this with a text of their own choosing.

These independence and stamina activities can be used at the beginning of the year to help students get into a habit of thinking about independent reading on a daily basis. It is also useful to revisit the activities with students who struggle so that you can monitor the texts they are reading and determine whether they need assistance in selecting appropriate independent-reading texts. Students who can effectively choose appropriate texts will be less likely to abandon books and more likely to spend time engaged in reading. They will become lifelong readers.

Activities:

Goal Post: Students build their stamina by increasing the amount of time they read, rather than the number of pages or books they read.
OBJECTIVE: *To increase independent reading stamina*
CCSS: RL/RI 3.10, 4.10, 5.10

Read It! Rate It!: Students decide whether they would recommend a text they have read to someone else.
OBJECTIVE: *To encourage analysis, response, and discussion of texts that students have read*
CCSS: RL/RI 3.10, 4.10, 5.10

Put Down That Book!: Students determine whether a short text is fiction or nonfiction. After reading the text, they reveal one thing they learned from the text. This reproducible would be suitable for the beginning of the year when students may be reading a variety of texts each day. It would also be useful for struggling readers who read a new text each day.
OBJECTIVES: *To read a variety of text types; to identify fiction and nonfiction texts; to organize information from various texts*
CCSS: RL/RI 3.10, 4.10, 5.10

Thumbs Up, Thumbs Down: Students record the title, author, and genre and give their opinion of several texts.
OBJECTIVES: *To think about different genres; to give an opinion about a text*
CCSS: RL/RI 3.10, 4.10, 5.10

Predict & Reflect: Students make predictions about a text. Students reading a longer chapter book may make predictions about what they will read the following day, and those completing a text in one sitting can record some sort of response to the text. As they continue to read, they evaluate their predictions. *Note:* You may need to duplicate more than one activity sheet to send home with students.
OBJECTIVES: *To make predictions; to reflect on predictions; to respond to text*
CCSS: RL 3.1, 3.10, 4.1, 4.10, 5.1, 5.10

My Reading Diary: Students reflect on the text they have read. This reproducible can be used with both literature and informational texts throughout the year. It encourages students to connect their reading to their own lives in some way—whether it is a personal connection, questions that arise, or thinking about what they read to comprehend the text.
OBJECTIVE: *To encourage students to think about a text in a variety of ways, such as personal connection, questioning, retelling, summarizing, and learning information*
CCSS: RL/RI 3.1, 3.10, 4.1, 4.10, 5.1, 5.10

Choose Your Book: Students think about why they chose to read a particular text. This activity can be revisited several times throughout the year, especially for those students who find it difficult to choose books that correspond to their interests and reading level.
OBJECTIVE: *To analyze personal reading preferences and habits*
CCSS: RL/RI 3.10, 4.10, 5.10

Name _____ Date _____

Goal Post

Setting a goal for reading can motivate you to read more. Every minute you spend reading makes you a better reader! Set a goal for how many minutes you will read this week.

Record what you read and how long you read each day. You may read several books each day or read a longer book for the week.

MY GOAL ⌐ I want to read for _____ minutes by the end of the week.

DAY	TITLE	AUTHOR	NUMBER OF MINUTES
Monday			
Tuesday			
Wednesday			
Thursday			
Friday			
		TOTAL NUMBER OF MINUTES	

MY NEW GOAL ⌐ Next week, I want to read for _____ minutes by the end of the week.

Reflect on your reading.

Did you reach your goal? Check a box. ☐ **YES** ☐ **NO**

If you didn't reach your goal, explain why. _____

_____

What can you try differently next week to meet your new goal? _____

_____

Name _____ Date _____

Read It! Rate It!

When you rate a book, think about these questions:

★ *How interesting was the book?*

★ *Would you recommend the book to someone else?*

Record each book that you read in the chart. Then use the following scale to rate it:

1	2	3	4
I didn't enjoy the book.	The book was okay, but I wouldn't recommend it.	I enjoyed the book, and I would recommend it.	This was a fantastic book, and I want to read it again!

TITLE	AUTHOR	NUMBER OF PAGES	DATE I BEGAN	DATE I FINISHED	MY RATING

Name _____ Date _____

Put Down That Book!

Everyone loves a good book, but this isn't the only way to read. Reading material is all around you. You can read short books, blogs, magazines, manuals, and even food containers in one sitting.

Select a short text that will take you about 10 minutes to read. Then complete the chart.

	TITLE & AUTHOR	I CHOSE IT BECAUSE . . .	I FOUND IT . . .	FICTION OR NONFICTION?	ONE THING I LEARNED . . .
MONDAY					
TUESDAY					
WEDNESDAY					
THURSDAY					
FRIDAY					

Name _____

Date _____

Thumbs Up, Thumbs Down

Reading about a topic across different genres builds your knowledge.

When you finish a book, record the genre and whether you liked it.

EXAMPLES OF GENRES

Nonfiction:	**Fiction:**	
All About Books	Science Fiction	Short Stories
How-To	Mystery	Fairy Tales
Biography	Fantasy	Poetry
Question-and-Answer	Folktales	Historical Fiction
Poetry	Realistic Fiction	

TITLE / AUTHOR	GENRE	CHECK A BOX. THEN EXPLAIN WHY YOU FEEL THAT WAY ABOUT THE BOOK.	
		☐ 👍	☐ 👎
		☐ 👍	☐ 👎
		☐ 👍	☐ 👎
		☐ 👍	☐ 👎

Share your thumbs-up books with your friends at school.

Predict & Reflect

When readers enjoy what they read, they wonder what will happen next. They predict what will happen to the characters, how the characters will react, and how the story will end.

Record the title and author of the book you are reading. In the chart below, record the number of pages you read each day. Then, after you read, make a prediction about what you think will happen next in the book. After you've read further, reflect on your earlier predictions.

Title: _____   Author: _____

DATE	PAGES READ		PREDICT AND REFLECT
	FROM	TO	
			My prediction is: My prediction was correct/incorrect because: How this prediction helped me understand the book:
			My prediction is: My prediction was correct/incorrect because: How this prediction helped me understand the book:

My Reading Diary

Strong readers are always thinking as they read. They reflect on their feelings. They make connections. They ask questions. They think about the interesting information they're learning.

Keep a record of the texts you read this week. After you read a text, think about it. Then write your thoughts in the diary.

Dear Diary,

Today is (date): _____

I read (title): _____

by (author): _____

Here are my thoughts about it:

WHAT YOU MIGHT THINK ABOUT . . .

★ *What connection can I make to this book?*

★ *What did this book make me think about?*

★ *What other text does it remind me of?*

★ *What questions do I have about it?*

★ *What did I learn?*

★ *How would I summarize this book?*

ANYTHING AT ALL!

Name _____ Date _____

Choose Your Book

Readers choose texts for many reasons. Here are a few reasons:

- ★ *They can read the text.*
- ★ *A friend told them to read it.*
- ★ *They want to read about a specific topic.*
- ★ *They are rereading it because they like it so much.*

Choose a text and tell why you chose it.

Title: _____ Author: _____

I chose this text because _____

_____

_____

_____

Tell whether you understand what you read. _____

_____

_____

Tell whether you wanted to keep reading it. _____

_____

_____

Was this text right for you? Mark the scale below.

1   2   3   4   5

No!   *It was okay.*   *Yes!*

Reading Strategies: Overview

We teach many different reading strategies to students, such as predicting, visualizing, making connections, summarizing, and making inferences. They must practice these strategies at home. Students not only use these strategies before reading an independent text, but they also use the strategies during and after reading to comprehend the text. We want students to apply reading strategies as naturally as they absorb challenging texts. The following activities help students practice all the ways that lifelong readers negotiate and navigate text.

Activities:

Crystal Ball Predictions: Students use a variety of pre-reading strategies to make predictions about a story. Then they revisit predictions and examine them for accuracy.
OBJECTIVES: *To make predictions using text features; to analyze those predictions by comparing them to what actually happened in the story*
CCSS: RL 3.1, 3.10, 4.1, 4.10, 5.1, 5.10

The Next Chapter: This activity is done with a chapter book. Students make and reflect on predictions about the upcoming chapter.
OBJECTIVE: *To use chapter titles, plot information, and character analysis to make thoughtful predictions*
CCSS: RL 3.1, 3.10, 4.1, 4.10, 5.1, 5.10

Character Clues: Students think about the feelings of a character they have read about. They use this knowledge to make predictions about what will happen in the text.
OBJECTIVE: *To analyze and make inferences about the feelings and actions of a character*
CCSS: RL 3.3, 3.10, 4.3, 4.10, 5.3, 5.10

I Wonder . . . : Students write questions before reading a text. After reading, they answer these questions and ask new ones that arose during reading.
OBJECTIVE: *To use questions as a tool for understanding before, during, and after reading*
CCSS: RL 3.1, 3.10, 4.1, 4.10, 5.1, 5.10

Friendly Qs: Students think of strong open-ended questions to ask others in a discussion of texts. They can be reading the same text or different texts.
OBJECTIVE: *To ask open-ended questions to a partner*
CCSS: RL 3.1, 3.10, 4.1, 4.10, 5.1, 5.10

TV Scene Sketch: This activity should be used with texts that are not illustrated. Students visualize what they have read and make a sketch of the scene as though it were happening on TV.
OBJECTIVE: *To deepen understanding by visualizing a scene from a text in order to summarize the scene*
CCSS: RL 3.2, 3.10, 4.2, 4.10, 5.2, 5.10

That Reminds Me . . . : Students liken their experiences to a text they are reading, then explain how these experiences helped them understand the text.
OBJECTIVE: *To deepen understanding and interest by making a personal connection to a text*
CCSS: RL 3.3, 3.10, 4.3, 4.10, 5.3, 5.10

Compare and Contrast Across Texts: Students think about texts they have previously read, then reflect on how ideas from those texts help them understand a text they are currently reading.
OBJECTIVE: *To use other texts to improve comprehension*
CCSS: RL/RI 3.1, 3.9, 3.10, 4.1, 4.9, 4.10, 5.1, 5.9, 5.10

Go Global: Students make a connection between a text and past and present world events.
OBJECTIVE: *To connect the text to real-life events*
CCSS: RL/RI 3.1, 3.6, 3.10, 4.1, 4.6, 4.10, 5.1, 5.6, 5.10

Only Connect!: Students describe how a text relates to another text, their own life, and past and present world events.
OBJECTIVE: *To connect a text to multiple aspects of a student's experience*
CCSS: RL/RI 3.1, 3.6, 3.10, 4.1, 4.6, 4.10, 5.1, 5.6, 5.10

Somebody . . . Wanted . . . But . . . So . . . : Students use their knowledge of story elements to summarize a text.
OBJECTIVE: *To use story elements to summarize*
CCSS: RL 3.2, 3.3, 3.10, 4.2, 4.3, 4.10, 5.2, 5.3, 5.10

Text Message Summary: Students write a short, concise summary of a text.
OBJECTIVE: *To encourage students to focus on the essential details of a text*
CCSS: RL/RI 3.2, 3.10, 4.2, 4.10, 5.2, 5.10

What's It All About?: Students use quotes from a text to make inferences about its theme.
OBJECTIVE: *To analyze quotes for deeper understanding of theme*
CCSS: RL 3.1, 3.2, 3.10, 4.1, 4.2, 4.10, 5.1, 5.2, 5.10

Character Trading Card: Students create a trading card for a character based on their reading.
OBJECTIVE: *To make inferences about several aspects of a character based on information from the text*
CCSS: RL 3.3, 3.10, 4.3, 4.10, 5.3, 5.10

Name _____ Date _____

Crystal Ball Predictions

When you read, you make predictions about the text. You may use the title, illustrations or pictures, a blurb on the back cover, comments from friends, other texts by the same author, or what you know about the topic or genre to make these predictions.

Before you begin reading, make two predictions about your text and write them in the crystal balls.

Title: _____ Author: _____

When you finish reading, look at your predictions.

Were your predictions correct? ☐ **YES** ☐ **NO**

If they were not correct, explain why. _____

_____

_____

How did your predictions help as you read? _____

_____

_____

_____

Name _____ Date _____

The Next Chapter

Title: _____ Author: _____

Strong readers make predictions before they begin reading a chapter. They do this by—

★ *looking at the title of the chapter*

★ *thinking about the last chapter they read*

★ *reflecting on what they know about the characters or big ideas in the book*

Then they make a guess about what will happen.

BEFORE READING the next chapter, make a prediction about what will happen. Use text evidence to support your prediction.

_____

_____

_____

_____

_____

_____

AFTER READING, tell whether your prediction was correct.   ☐ YES   ☐ NO

What do you predict will happen in the next chapter? Use text evidence to support your prediction.

_____

_____

_____

_____

_____

Name _____ Date _____

Character Clues

Title: _____ Author: _____

Readers think about what the character says and does to help them understand the text. This helps them make predictions about what might happen.

Complete the activity.

1. Who is the main character in your book? _____

2. Wherever you are in your reading, stop and think about what is happening to that character.

3. Think about how he or she might be feeling.

4. Draw a picture of how you think the character might be feeling.

Based on how the character feels, what do you think is going to happen next?

_____

_____

Name _____ Date _____

I Wonder . . .

Title: _____ Author: _____

Readers ask questions before, during, and after reading. They might ask questions about these and other things:

- ★ *a fact they want to know*
- ★ *a plot element they are wondering about*
- ★ *a book's big idea*

BEFORE READING: Write down questions you have about the text.

DURING READING: Write down any new questions that arise as you read and the answers you find to your questions.

??? QUESTIONS ???	!!! ANSWERS !!!
1.	
2.	
3.	
4.	

AFTER READING: Write down any new questions you have.

1.	
2.	**?**
3.	
4.	

Name _____ Date _____

Friendly Qs

Title: _____ Author: _____

Readers like to discuss books with others. They ask each other questions.

What do the characters do that make them seem real and believable?

What is something you really want to know?

How has the book changed your thinking?

What do you like about your book so far?

What is your favorite part of the book?

Think of three great questions to ask your book club/partner.

1.

2.

3.

HINT: Did you notice something about the questions? None of them can be answered with a yes or a no.

Name _____ Date _____

TV Scene Sketch

Title: _____ Author: _____

Readers visualize pictures in their heads to go with the words in a text. They imagine the people and places described by the author. They think about what the words make them see, hear, taste, smell, and feel.

Choose a scene or a passage from your book. Draw it on the TV screen.

Write two or three sentences to explain what is happening on the screen.

_____

_____

_____

Name _____ Date _____

That Reminds Me . . .

Title: _____ Author: _____

Readers often connect their reading to their lives. They may connect:

★ *a character to themselves or someone in their own life*

★ *the setting to a place they've visited*

★ *an event to an experience they've had*

Write about a connection that you have to a character, a setting, or an event in your book.

How did this connection help you better understand the story?

_____

_____

_____

Name _____ Date _____

Compare and Contrast Across Texts

Title: _____ Author: _____

Readers make connections across the many kinds of reading they do. They compare a book to a poem or a chapter book to another chapter book. They compare the following elements:

★ *genre:* Are both texts fiction?

★ *authors:* Which point of view does each author use to tell the story?

★ *similar characters, events, or big ideas:* How are they alike? How are they different?

Compare your book to another text you have read. Write the title and author below.

Title: _____ Author: _____

Which elements are similar? Which elements are different? Complete the Venn diagram to compare the two texts.

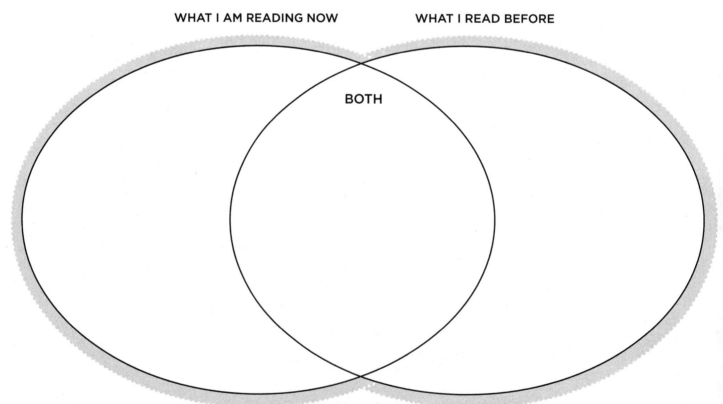

WHAT I AM READING NOW   WHAT I READ BEFORE

BOTH

How does this Venn diagram help you understand the text you are reading now?

_____

_____

Name _____ Date _____

Go Global

Title: _____ Author: _____

Readers often make connections between the text they are reading and something that is happening or has happened in the world. The text might be a newspaper or magazine article, an informational text about a specific topic or event, or a story on the television or radio.

As you read, think about the text-to-world connection that you are making. How are the events in this story similar to things that happen in the real world?

MY BOOK	THE WORLD
When I read the part about . . .	It reminded me of . . .

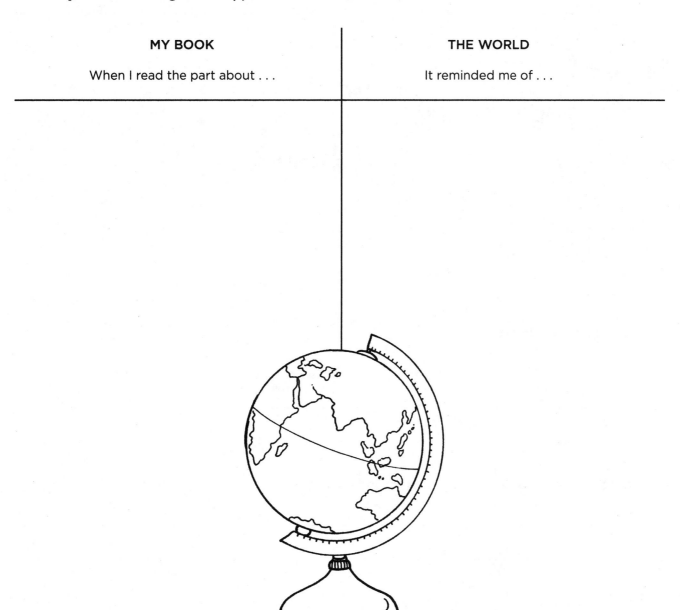

Name _____ Date _____

Only Connect!

Title: _____ Author: _____

Readers make different types of connections to the reading they do to help them understand what they have read.

Think about connections you have made. Have you connected your reading to your own life, another book, or something or someone in the world? Check one or more of the boxes below.

☐ MY OWN LIFE	☐ ANOTHER BOOK	☐ THE WORLD

Describe the connection(s). _____

_____

_____

_____

How did the connection(s) help you understand your reading? _____

_____

_____

_____

_____

Name _____ Date _____

Somebody ... Wanted ... But ... So ...

Title: _____ Author: _____

Readers often summarize what they've read to make sure they understand a story and to share information. They use their understanding of these story elements to write a summary:

★ *character*

★ *problem: what's getting in the character's way*

★ *goal: what the character wants*

★ *solution: how the character solves this problem*

Write a summary of your text.

SOMEBODY (character)

WANTED (goal)

BUT (problem)

SO (solution)

Name _____ Date _____

Text Message Summary

Title: _____ Author: _____

Readers often summarize what they have read. This helps them remember the most important ideas in the text.

After reading your text, think about what you could tell a friend about it. Summarize the book in a text message of 140 characters (letters). Remember to include the character(s), goal, problem, and solution.

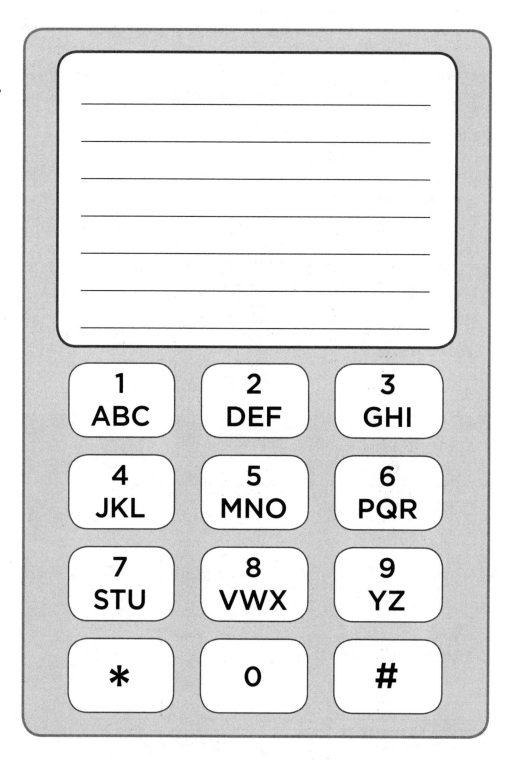

Name _____ Date _____

What's It All About?

Title: _____ Author: _____

An author doesn't always state the theme of a text. Readers often must make an inference about the theme. They draw a conclusion based on what happens in the text.

Write one or more quotes from your book in the left column of the chart. Choose quotes that you think show the theme of the text. In the right column, write what each quote tells you about the theme.

QUOTE	INFERENCE

Name _____ Date _____

Character Trading Card

Title: _____ Author: _____

Authors don't tell readers everything about a character. They write stories so readers can figure out what type of person a character is. Authors give clues so readers can make inferences about a character's personality.

Choose a character from your text: _____

Think about what you know about this character. Then make a trading card for the character. Draw a picture of the character on the front of the card and write his or her name. On the back, write details about the character. You can include any nicknames, physical details (what he or she looks like), personality traits (what type of person he or she is), and the character's feelings and actions.

(front)   (back)

Literary Elements: Overview

Many of the skills that we ask students to focus on are related to literary elements. The following activities will show students' understanding of literary elements by asking them to retell stories in a variety of ways, connecting what they read to themselves and other texts, and using higher-level thinking skills to interpret what the author is saying. Rather than answering simple comprehension questions, students show their understanding of literary elements by completing these fun and engaging activities after their reading.

Activities:

Story Web: Students identify the elements of a story: characters, setting, problem, and solution.
  OBJECTIVES: *To demonstrate understanding of story elements; to organize ideas from a story*
  CCSS: RL 3.2, 3.9, 3.10, 4.2, 4.9, 4.10, 5.2, 5.9, 5.10

The Three Steps: Students record sequence of events including key details such as characters, setting, problem, and solution.
  OBJECTIVE: *To organize key information from a story*
  CCSS: RL 3.2, 3.10, 4.2, 4.10, 5.2, 5.10

Cartoon Sequencing: Students record sequence of events using pictures and speech bubbles.
  OBJECTIVE: *To synthesize information by creating an illustration*
  CCSS: RL 3.2, 3.10, 4.2, 4.10, 5.2, 5.10

Focus on Character: Students choose and describe a character using evidence from the text.
  OBJECTIVES: *To describe a character's physical and personality traits; to use text evidence to support thinking*
  CCSS: RL 3.3, 3.5, 3.10, 4.3, 4.5, 4.10, 5.3, 5.5, 5.10

Stuck on a Desert Island: Students show their understanding of a character.
  OBJECTIVES: *To demonstrate knowledge of a character; to make inferences about a character*
  CCSS: RL 3.1, 3.3, 3.5, 3.10, 4.1, 4.3, 4.5, 4.10, 5.1, 5.3, 5.5, 5.10

We Have So Much in Common: Students compare and contrast themselves to a character.
  OBJECTIVES: *To make connections to a character; to record information in a Venn diagram or another graphic organizer*
  CCSS: RL 3.3, 3.5, 3.10, 4.3, 4.5, 4.10, 5.3, 5.5, 5.10

I Friend You: Students compare and contrast two characters. Then they decide which character they would like to have as a friend and why. This guides students to analyze their knowledge of the character and to support their opinion.
  OBJECTIVES: *To compare two characters; to use textual evidence to express an opinion about a character; to analyze knowledge of a character*
  CCSS: RL 3.1, 3.3, 3.9, 3.10, 4.1, 4.3, 4.9, 4.10, 5.1, 5.3, 5.9, 5.10

Let Me Introduce You: Students choose two characters from different texts and think about how the characters would interact.
  OBJECTIVES: *To compare characters across texts; to analyze knowledge of two or more characters from different texts*
  CCSS: RL 3.1, 3.3 3.9, 3.10, 4.1, 4.3, 4.9, 4.10, 5.1, 5.3, 5.9, 5.10

Changes in Character: Students choose a character and think about how he or she changes throughout the text and what caused the change to occur.

  OBJECTIVE: *To analyze dynamic characters from a text*
  CCSS: RL 3.1, 3.3, 3.5, 3.10, 4.1, 4.3, 4.5, 4.10, 5.1, 5.3, 5.5, 5.10

Picture Postcard: Students think about the major setting of an illustrated text, describe it in their own words, and illustrate it. Use this homework page with students who are reading texts with picture clues.
  OBJECTIVE: *To use picture clues to describe a setting*
  CCSS: RL 3.1, 3.7, 3.10, 4.1, 4.7, 4.10, 5.1, 5.7, 5.10

Be the Illustrator: Students describe the setting and then draw how they imagine it looks. Students should select a book that is not illustrated for this activity.
  OBJECTIVE: *To convert descriptive language into an illustration*
  CCSS: RL 3.1, 3.10, 4.1, 4.10, 5.1, 5.10

Theme Talk: Students create a symbol to represent a theme in their text.
  OBJECTIVES: *To infer theme; to record thoughts about a text*
  CCSS: RL 3.2, 3.10, 4.2, 4.10, 5.2, 5.10

Theme Symbol: Students create a symbol to represent a theme in their text. This allows them to synthesize the information from the text and represent it in a creative way.
  OBJECTIVES: *To identify the theme of a text; to creatively represent the theme of a text with an illustration or graphic*
  CCSS: RL 3.2, 3.10, 4.2, 4.10, 5.2, 5.10

Theme Time Line: Students think about how the theme of their text unfolds. They then create a series of illustrations to show the development of the theme. Students demonstrate a true understanding of the text and use text evidence to support their idea.
  OBJECTIVE: *To infer theme*
  CCSS: RL 3.2, 3.10, 4.2, 4.10, 5.2, 5.10

Start Your Engines: Students reflect on the beginning of a text—what is surprising, what questions they have, and what immediately captures their attention.
  OBJECTIVES: *To analyze the beginning of a text; to develop better understanding of a text through close reading*
  CCSS: RL 3.1, 3.6, 3.10, 4.1, 4.6, 4.10, 5.1, 5.6, 5.10

Crossing the Finish Line: Students express their opinion about the ending of a text and then write a different, yet suitable, ending.
  OBJECTIVES: *To analyze the end of a text; to use imagination and opinion to rewrite the end of a text*
  CCSS: RL 3.1, 3.6, 3.10, 4.1, 4.6, 4.10, 5.1, 5.6, 5.10

Name _____ Date _____

Story Web

Title: _____ Author: _____

All stories always have the following elements:

★ characters   ★ setting   ★ problem   ★ solution

Readers identify these story elements as they read. This strategy helps them remember the story and make connections to other stories.

Complete the web for the elements in your book.

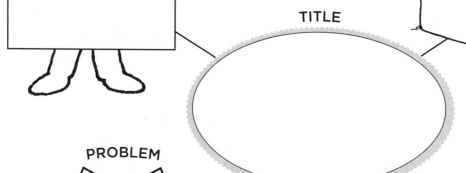

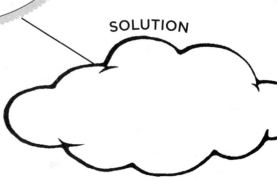

Does this story remind you of another story? Write the title and author below. Then describe the connection on the back of this sheet.

Title: _____ Author: _____

Name _____ Date _____

The Three Steps

Title: _____ Author: _____

At the beginning of a story, the author introduces readers to the character(s) and the setting. In the middle, readers find out what the problem is and how the character(s) tries to solve the problem. Everything is usually wrapped up at the end of the story.

Record the sequence of events in your story. Be sure to include the main characters, setting, problem, and solution.

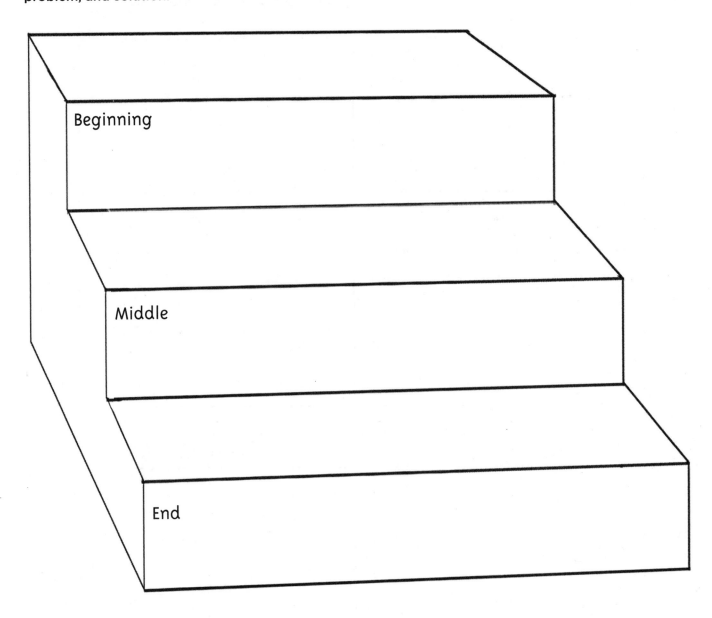

Beginning

Middle

End

Name _____ Date _____

Cartoon Sequencing

Title: _____ Author: _____

It is important to know the sequence, or order, in which the events take place in a story. This helps readers understand what they read.

Draw cartoons to record the sequence of events in your story. Be sure to include the characters, setting, problem, and solution. Don't forget some speech bubbles to show dialogue!

BEGINNING	NEXT

THEN	NEXT

THEN	FINALLY

Name _____ Date _____

Focus on Character

Title: _____ Author: _____

Authors give clues about characters through dialogue and the way characters interact.

Choose one of the characters from your story: _____

What does the character look like? What type of person is the character? Use evidence from the text to support your descriptions.

Describe your character's physical traits. (*What does the character look like?*)	Evidence from the text:	Describe the character's personality traits. (*What type of person is the character?*)	Evidence from the text:

Draw a picture of the character.

Stuck on a Desert Island

Title: _____ Author: _____

Authors want readers to get to know the characters they write about.

Choose one of the characters from your book: _____

Think of three to six objects the character would take to a desert island. Draw them on the island.

Identify each object. Then explain why your character would take each object.

1	2	3
4	5	6

Name _____ Date _____

We Have So Much in Common

Title: _____ Author: _____

Readers often make personal connections to characters in a book.

Compare one of the characters in the book to yourself.

BOTH OF US

CHARACTER

ME

Name _____ Date _____

I Friend You

~~~~~~~~~~~~~~~~~~~~~~~~~~~~~~

Title: _____ Author: _____

Authors have characters interact with each other to keep their stories moving forward.

Think about what you know about two characters from your story.

Character 1: _____ Character 2: _____

Tell how the characters are similar and different. Think about their actions, words, thoughts, and feelings.

The characters are similar to each other because:

The characters are different from each other because:

I would rather have _____ **(name of character) as my friend because:**

Let Me Introduce You

~~~~~~

Title: _____ Author: _____

It can be fun to imagine how characters from different texts might interact with each other.

Think about a character from the book you are reading: _____

Now think of a character from a different book.

Title: _____ Character: _____

Sketch the two characters and where and how they might meet. Write a conversation between them that shows who they are. Use speech bubbles.

Name _____ Date _____

Changes in Character

Title: _____ Author: _____

Something often happens in stories to make characters change. For example, they might:

- ★ *learn something*
- ★ *get or lose something*
- ★ *experience something*
- ★ *change their minds about something*

Think of a character from your story: _____

Describe how this character changes in the story.

At the beginning of the story, the character:
At the end of the story, the character:
How did the character change between the beginning and the end of the story?
Why did the character change?

Picture Postcard

~~~~~~~~~~~~~~~~~~~~~~~~~~~~~~~~~~~~~~~

Title: _____ Author: _____

The setting is where and when the story takes place. This can change many times throughout a text. The illustrator gives readers many clues about the setting through pictures.

Look at the pictures in the text. Use them to describe the setting at the beginning of the book.

_____

_____

_____

_____

_____

Draw a postcard of this setting.

Name _____ Date _____

Be the Illustrator

Title: _____ Author: _____

Texts don't always show pictures of the setting. Readers must imagine what the setting would look like based on the author's description.

Find the words the author uses to describe the setting of your book. Write them below.

Now draw a picture of how you imagine the setting based on the words of the author.

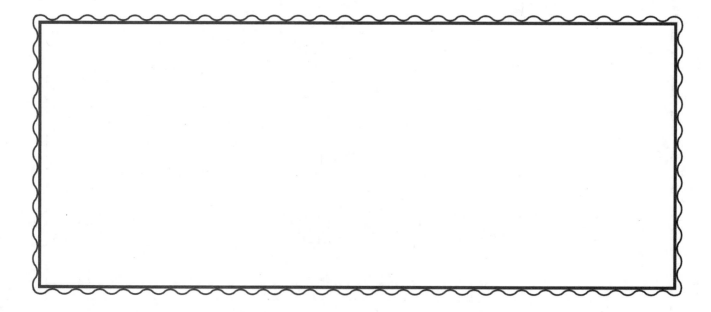

Name _____ Date _____

Theme Talk

~~~~~~~~~~~~~~~~~~~~~~~

Title: _____ Author: _____

The theme of a story or a book is its message about life. Some examples of themes are friendship, courage, hope, justice, human nature, life, and love.

Write a short summary of the story or book.

SUMMARY

What is the theme of the story or book? What did the author want you to learn?

THEME

Name _____ Date _____

Theme Symbol

Title: _____ Author: _____

Readers think about theme as they read. It's fun to think of a symbol to go with the theme. For example, you could draw two hands clasped together to show the theme of friendship.

Identify one theme from a chapter or the book: _____

Create a symbol that represents this theme.

Explain why you chose this symbol. _____

_____

_____

Theme Time Line

~~~~~~~~~~~~~~~~~~~~~~~~~~~

Title: _____ Author: _____

Many authors let their theme unfold throughout the text. They leave clues to help readers determine the theme.

Draw pictures to represent the theme as it unfolds in the story. Example theme: *Friendship*

- **First, the character is lonely** (*draw one person*).
- **Next, the character realizes it is important to have a friend** (*draw the character reaching out*).
- **Finally, the character finds a friend and is not lonely anymore** (*draw two friends together*).

What do you think the main theme of your text is? _____

_____

FIRST   NEXT   FINALLY

Name _____ Date _____

Start Your Engines

Title: _____ Author: _____

Readers often read the beginning of a book to help them decide whether to choose it, so authors try to make the beginning interesting. Authors might do the following:

- ★ *introduce an interesting setting*
- ★ *start with dialogue*
- ★ *begin in the middle of the action*

Reread the first paragraph of your book. Then copy it below.

_____

_____

_____

_____

_____

_____

What feels surprising, interesting, or captures your attention in this paragraph? _____

_____

_____

_____

Name _____ Date _____

Crossing the Finish Line

Title: _____ Author: _____

Readers pay special attention to the end of stories. Some endings wrap everything up. Others show the feelings of the characters. Sometimes an author shares a final deep thought or leaves you with questions.

After finishing your book, answer the questions below.

How did the text end?

How did you feel about the ending? Why?

How else could the story have ended? Write a different ending to the story.

Informational Text: Overview

Today, students are asked to read more and more in the content areas. With such easy access to information, it is imperative that we teach students how to understand and analyze information from a variety of different sources. The activities in this section challenge students to read and interpret information in an engaging way. They encourage students to think about how the information is presented, then collect and present it in different ways.

Activities:

Fact Features: Students focus on different text features in their informational text and reflect on how these features may help them while they are reading.
OBJECTIVE: *To encourage close reading and analyzing of textual elements*
CCSS: RI 3.1, 3.5, 3.10, 4.1, 4.10, 5.1, 5.10

Information Sparklers: Students gather and record interesting and important facts from informational text.
OBJECTIVES: *To understand the difference between important and interesting information; to organize ideas from informational text*
CCSS: RI 3.1, 3.3, 3.7, 3.10, 4.1, 4.3, 4.7, 4.10, 5.1, 5.3, 5.7, 5.10

What's Big? What's Small?: Students identify the main idea of a text, then record details that support it.
OBJECTIVE: *To differentiate between a main idea and supporting details in a text*
CCSS: RI 3.1, 3.2, 3.7, 3.10, 4.1, 4.2, 4.7, 4.10, 5.1, 5.2, 5.10

Important Decisions: Students locate important information in their text and explain why it is essential.
OBJECTIVES: *To locate important information in a text; to use textual information to justify an opinion*
CCSS: RI 3.1, 3.8, 3.10, 4.1, 4.8, 4.10, 5.1, 5.8, 5.10

Biography Time Line: Students use the information from a biography to create a time line showing important events in that person's life.
OBJECTIVE: *To locate main ideas and identify important information in a biography*
CCSS: RI 3.1, 3.7, 3.10, 4.1, 4.7, 4.10, 5.1, 5.7, 5.10

Everyone Has an Opinion: Students identify the author's point of view in an informational text and then write their own opinion on the subject.
OBJECTIVES: *To identify an author's point of view; to express a personal opinion; to compare and contrast one's own opinion with the author's*
CCSS: RI 3.1, 3.6, 3.10, 4.1, 4.6, 4.10, 5.1, 5.6, 5.10

Fact Families: Students classify information from an informational text into categories that make sense to them.
OBJECTIVE: *To analyze and organize facts from an informational text*
CCSS: RI 3.1, 3.5, 3.7, 3.10, 4.1, 4.5, 4.7, 4.10, 5.1, 5.10

Information Insights: Students use information they've learned from a text to create an illustration, chart, or graph.
OBJECTIVE: *To demonstrate comprehension by creating a visual element*
CCSS: RI 3.1, 3.5, 3.7, 3.10, 4.1, 4.7, 4.10, 5.1, 5.7, 5.10

Thinking About Facts: Students use illustrations to record their thoughts about the facts in their reading.
OBJECTIVE: *To analyze and reflect on facts from an informational text*
CCSS: RI 3.1, 3.10, 4.1, 4.10, 5.1, 5.10

A Book Blurb: Students write a book blurb to entice others to read an informational text. In doing so, they convert information from one genre, informative, to another, persuasion.
OBJECTIVES: *To practice persuasive writing; to practice summarizing the main ideas of an informational text*
CCSS: RI 3.1, 3.2, 3.10, 4.1, 4.2, 4.10, 5.1, 5.2, 5.10

Name _____ Date _____

Fact Features

Title: _____ Author: _____

Authors can include many text features in informational texts. Headings, pictures, charts, maps, and captions make it easier for readers to locate information.

Preview your text. Describe the text features it contains in the chart below. Explain how each feature helps you understand the text.

TEXT FEATURES IN MY BOOK

Headings: This text feature is helpful because	**Subheadings:** This text feature is helpful because
Visuals: This text feature is helpful because	**Captions:** This text feature is helpful because
Tables/Charts: This text feature is helpful because	**Diagrams/Maps:** This text feature is helpful because

Information Sparklers

Title: _____ Author: _____

Informational texts give readers a lot of interesting facts about a subject. When good readers read informational texts with several new ideas, they think about which ideas are the most important.

After reading your informational text, think about which information is interesting and which is important.

What is the most important thing you learned? Tell why you think it is important.

_____

_____

_____

_____

_____

_____

_____

What is an interesting thing you learned? Tell why it is interesting to you.

_____

_____

_____

_____

_____

_____

_____

Name _____ Date _____

What's Big? What's Small?

Title: _____ Author: _____

The **MAIN IDEA** of a text is what it is mostly about. It is the idea that the author most wants you to understand when you read. **SUPPORTING DETAILS** tell more about the main idea. They help you better understand the main idea and why it is important.

After reading your text, fill in the graphic organizer.

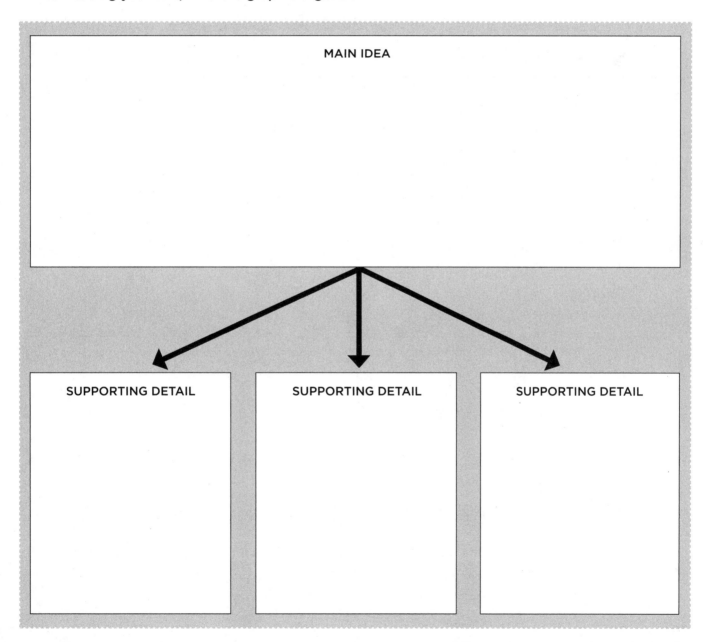

Important Decisions

Title: _____ Author: _____

Authors try to share important information about a topic in an interesting way. They may include photos or questions to capture readers' attention so they will read on to learn the important information.

In the chart below, write important information from your text, such as people, events, dates, or places. Explain why you think each is important.

This information is important . . .	It is important because . . .

Describe how the author presents this important information in an interesting way: Text features? Writing style? Other ways? _____

_____

_____

Name _____

Date _____

Biography Time Line

Title: _____   Author: _____

A biography gives readers important information about a person's life.

After reading a biography, choose five important details and dates. Record them on the time line below.

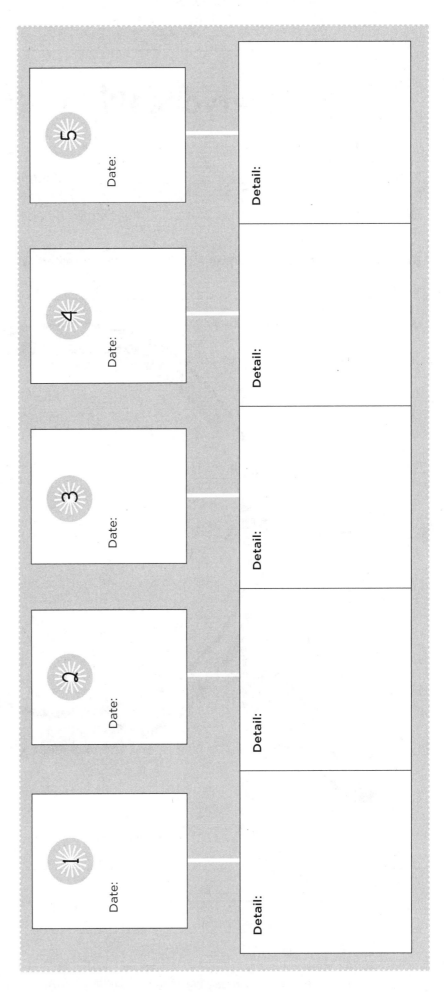

Everyone Has an Opinion

Title: _____ Author: _____

Every author has a point of view. This point of view may be about politics, history, a person, human nature, or a global issue.

Read an informational text about a topic you are interested in.

Topic: _____

What is the author's point of view?

What is your opinion about the topic? _____

_____

_____

_____

Name _____ Date _____

Fact Families

Title: _____ Author: _____

Informational texts can be organized in different ways. Headings and subheadings can help explain how an author has grouped facts. You can think of these groupings as fact families.

Create two fact families from your reading. Use headings and subheadings.

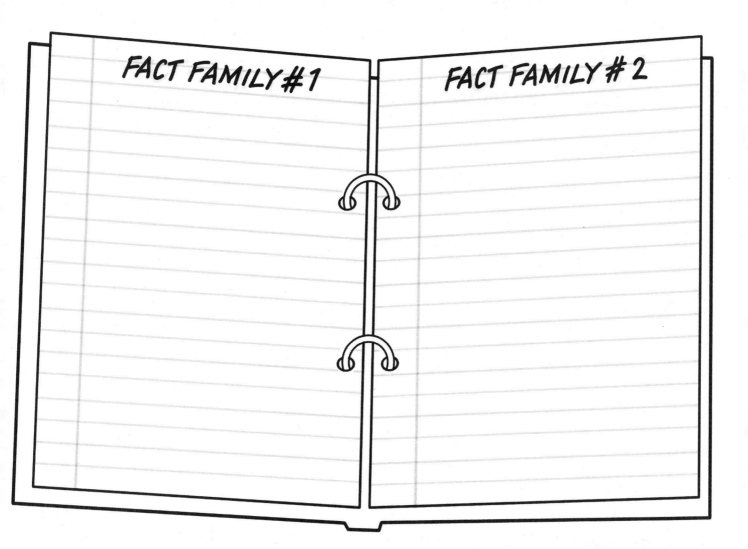

FACT FAMILY #1

FACT FAMILY #2

Name _____ Date _____

Information Insights

Title: _____ Author: _____

Readers learn facts about a topic from an informational text. Authors often include charts and/or diagrams to make facts easy to understand.

How would you teach someone about a fact that you learned from your text? Create a diagram, chart, or illustration to help you do this. Include a caption that describes your diagram, chart, or illustration.

Fact: _____

Caption: _____

_____

Name _____ Date _____

Thinking About Facts

Title: _____ Author: _____

Informational texts give readers facts about a topic. These facts often make us think, wonder why or how, or feel amazement.

Record and draw a picture of two facts from your reading. Then write what you think about each fact.

FACT #1	PICTURE #1

My Thinking: _____
_____
_____

FACT #2	PICTURE #2

My Thinking: _____
_____
_____

Name _____ Date _____

A Book Blurb

Title: _____ Author: _____

Authors of informational texts inform readers of facts about a topic. Short statements—blurbs— often appear on the back cover of a book. Book blurbs entice the reader by giving a snapshot of what to expect from the text.

Think about the text you read. What did you learn about the topic? Write a short blurb to entice other readers to read the text. Be sure to include the title and the author.

Genre: Overview

Students must read widely and deeply from many genres to prepare themselves for their future. Through extensive readings from a variety of texts, they will gain knowledge of different text structures and be able to interpret many different kinds of literary texts. The following fun activities support these skills by allowing students to choose their own texts within a specific genre and showing that they understand the characteristics and key ideas of that genre.

Activities:

Pinpoint Genre: Students identify the genre of their text and explain the characteristics of that genre.

> OBJECTIVES: *To categorize texts by genre; to use textual evidence to explain a genre*
>
> CCSS: RL/RI: 3.4, 3.5, 3.10, 4.4, 4.5, 4.10, 5.4, 5.5, 5.10

Genre Racetrack: Students are encouraged to read a broad range of texts. This activity is especially beneficial for students who read only one genre since they must read different genres to reach the finish line.

> OBJECTIVE: *To read a variety of text types*
>
> CCSS: RL/RI: 3.4, 3.10, 4.4, 4.10, 5.4, 5.10

Genre Bingo: Students are encouraged to read a variety of genres over a period of time. You may have students complete a row horizontally, vertically, or diagonally, or complete the entire bingo card.

> OBJECTIVE: *To read a variety of text types*
>
> CCSS: RL/RI: 3.4, 3.10, 4.4, 4.10, 5.4, 5.10

Another Time and Place: After reading historical fiction, students decide whether they would have liked to live during that time period, citing evidence from the text to support their opinion.

> OBJECTIVES: *To express an opinion and support it with details from text; to form opinions about plot and characters*
>
> CCSS: RL/RI: 3.1, 3.4, 3.6, 3.10, 4.1, 4.4, 4.6, 4.10, 5.1, 4.4, 5.6, 5.10; RI: 3.8, 4.8, 5.8

Fable Fun: Students reflect on a fable, focusing on an animal character.

> OBJECTIVES: *To state the moral or lesson of a fable; to support an opinion with textual details*
>
> CCSS: RL 3.2–3.4, 3.10, 4.2–4.4, 4.10, 5.2–5.4, 5.10

Myth Wanted Poster: Students design a Wanted poster for one of the characters from a myth.

> OBJECTIVE: *To demonstrate knowledge of a character from a myth*
>
> CCSS: RL 3.2–3.4, 3.10, 4.2–4.4, 4.10, 5.2–5.4, 5.10

Fantasy Bookmark: As students read their fantasy text, they find examples of the genre's key characteristics and mark page numbers where appropriate.

> OBJECTIVE: *To deepen comprehension of the fantasy genre*
>
> CCSS: RL 3.1–3.4, 3.10, 4.1–4.4, 4.10, 5.1–5.4, 5.10

Mystery Case File: Students keep track of what is happening in a mystery.

> OBJECTIVES: *To record and organize information during reading; to deepen understanding of the mystery genre*
>
> CCSS: RL 3.1–3.4, 3.10, 4.1–4.4, 4.10, 5.1–5.4, 5.10

Name _____ Date _____

Pinpoint Genre

Title: _____ Author: _____

There are a variety of genres that readers can explore. Here is a list of some genres.

FICTION	NONFICTION
Science fiction	All-About Books
Mystery	How-to Books
Fantasy	Biographies
Folktales	Question-and-Answer
Fairy tales	Poetry
Realistic fiction	
Historical fiction	
Short stories	
Poetry	

After reading your text, answer the questions below.

Which genre is your book? _____

How do you know? Which characteristics of that genre does your text have?

_____

_____

_____

_____

_____

_____

_____

Genre Racetrack

Your goal is to cross the finish line of the racetrack.

Choose a book from each genre that you want to read. Then complete the racetrack square for each book. Write the title and author in the square.

START

Realistic Fiction

How-to

FINISH!

Fiction in a series

All-About

Nonfiction

Historical Fiction

Poetry

Fairy Tale

Narrative

Genre Bingo

Choose a book that you are interested in reading. After completing it, determine which genre it is. Then fill in the correct bingo card square with the title and author. Your goal is to do any or all of the these:

- read all the genres in one column
- read all the genres in a diagonal row
- read all the genres in one row
- blackout: read ALL the genres on the Bingo card

BINGO

HISTORICAL FICTION	NONFICTION	FANTASY	SPORTS FICTION
MYSTERY	POETRY	NARRATIVE	BIOGRAPHY
HOW-TO	FICTION	FOLK TALE	FICTION IN A SERIES
SCIENCE FICTION	FANTASY	PERSUASIVE	REALISTIC FICTION

Name

Another Time and Place

Title: _____

Author: _____

Historical fiction tells a story that is set in the past. Many settings and characters are real. The authors of historical fiction try to make history come alive for their readers.

After reading a historical fiction text, answer the questions.

What is the setting of this story? _____

I would or would not like to live during this time because _____

_____

These three details from the text helped me make my decision: _____

_____

Name _____ Date _____

Fable Fun

Title: _____ Author: _____

Fables teach a lesson and carry a message. They often have animals as characters. These animals usually speak and act like humans.

Think about one of the animal characters in your fable.

Animal character: _____

Character's name: _____

Draw the animal below.

Now think about the lesson or message of your fable. Write it below.

_____

_____

How did your animal character learn the lesson or message in your fable?

_____

_____

_____

Name _____ Date _____

Myth Wanted Poster

Title: _____ Author: _____

A myth is a traditional story that explains why things are the way they are today. Authors of myths try to explain mysteries, supernatural events, or cultural traditions. Myths often involve gods or other fantastic creatures.

Create a Wanted poster for one of the characters in your myth.

Describe the character by answering the following questions on your poster:

- **Is this character good or bad?**
- **What is the reward for capturing this character?**
- **Why is the character wanted?**
- **What does this character look like?**

Draw a picture of the character on your Wanted poster.

Name _____ Date _____

Fantasy Bookmark

Title: _____ Author: _____

A fantasy usually takes place in an imaginary time or place and involves magic.

As you read a fantasy text, complete the bookmark below. Don't forget to include page numbers.

Title: _____

Hero: _____

Enemy/Villain: _____

Fight between good and evil: page _____

Imaginary time or place: page _____

Quest or mystery to solve: page _____

Magical powers: page _____

Save world of men from evil: page _____

Time travel: page _____

Main character shows courage: page _____

Hero learns lesson: _____

_____

_____

_____

Name_____ Date _____

Mystery Case File

Title: _____ Author: _____

In a mystery, a character usually must use clues to solve a crime.

After reading a mystery, complete the Mystery Case File below.

Detective/Sleuth (*Who is trying to solve the crime?*): _____
_____

Crime/Disappearance/Mystery (*What is the problem?*): _____
_____

Witnesses (*Who saw what happened?*): _____
_____

Witness Reports (*What did each witness see?*): _____
_____
_____
_____

Suspects:_____
_____

Motives:_____
_____
_____

Clues/Evidence: _____
_____
_____

How was the case solved?_____
_____
_____

Reading Responses: Overview

One way students show their understanding of a text is by answering comprehension questions. In this section, we ask students to demonstrate their understanding through real-life activities, such as writing to a friend, creating an advertisement, and using text evidence to explain their thoughts about characters and text. These are the types of skills that encourage students to think more deeply about the texts they read rather than just the sequence of events.

Activities:

Letter to a Character: Students write a letter to a character from their text. You may guide students to connect with the character or use text evidence to form opinions about his or her actions.
OBJECTIVE: *To analyze and connect with a character from a text*
CCSS: RL 3.1, 3.3, 3.10, 4.1, 4.3, 4.10, 5.1, 5.3, 5.10

Character Stamp: Students use their knowledge of a character to create a stamp representing that character.
OBJECTIVES: *To analyze a character from the text; to create an illustration that represents that character's actions and traits*
CCSS: RL 3.3, 3.10, 4.3, 4.10, 5.3, 5.10

Character Playdate: Using knowledge about a character, students write a range of activities that they could do with that character.
OBJECTIVE: *To analyze and connect with a character from a text*
CCSS: RL 3.3, 3.10, 4.3, 4.10, 5.3, 5.10

My Opinion: Before, During, and After: Students form and justify their opinions of a text throughout the reading process.
OBJECTIVES: *To analyze personal opinions; to study how opinions change and develop over the course of the reading process*
CCSS: RL 3.5, 3.6, 4.5, 4.6, 5.5, 5.6; RI 3.6, 4.6, 5.6

My Favorite Part: Using key details from a text, students discuss their favorite part of a story.
OBJECTIVE: *To express an opinion supported by text evidence*
CCSS: RL 3.1, 3.5, 3.10, 4.1, 4.5, 4.10, 5.1, 5.5, 5.10

What a Character: Students choose a favorite character and explain their choice.
OBJECTIVE: *To analyze personal opinions*
CCSS: RL 3.1, 3.3, 3.10, 4.1, 4.3, 4.10, 5.1, 5.3, 5.10

Book Advertisement: Students choose a text and write an advertisement for it, thereby enhancing their persuasive-writing skills.
OBJECTIVE: *To write persuasively and concisely about a text*
CCSS: RL/RI 3.1, 3.2, 3.10, 4.1, 4.2, 4.10, 5.1, 5.2, 5.10

Read This Book!: Students write a letter to a friend recommending a text. This activity demonstrates students' knowledge of how to write a strong letter and how to use evidence from the text to persuade the reader.
OBJECTIVE: *To write persuasively about a text using textual evidence as support*
CCSS: RL 3.5, 3.7, 3.10, 4.5, 4.7, 4.10, 5.5, 5.7, 5.10

Author's Purpose: Students think about the author's purpose and use evidence from the text to support their idea.
OBJECTIVES: *To infer an author's purpose; to form an opinion based on text evidence*
CCSS: RL/RI 3.1, 3.6, 3.10, 4.1, 4.6, 4.10, 5.1, 5.6, 5.10; RI 3.8, 4.8, 5.8

Visualize the Poem: Students draw an image in response to a poem, then write about their illustration.
OBJECTIVES: *To respond to a text by creating a visual image; to reflect on a poem*
CCSS: RL 3.1, 3.4, 3.5, 3.10, 4.1, 4.4, 4.5, 4.10, 5.1, 5.4, 5.5, 5.10

Poetic Response: Students reflect on the main idea of a poem and use evidence to support their thinking. They express an opinion about the title and create a new one for the poem, again using evidence to support their thinking.
OBJECTIVES: *To identify the main idea; to use supporting evidence; to express an opinion*
CCSS: RL 3.1, 3.4, 3.5, 3.10, 4.1, 4.4, 4.5, 4.10, 5.1, 5.4, 5.5, 5.10

Name _____   Date _____

Letter to a Character

Title: _____   Author: _____

Authors try to make their characters seem real and believable. Sometimes, readers wish they could communicate with the characters.

Write a letter to a character from your text. You can write about anything. You might let the character know how you feel about his or her actions toward other characters or share a similar experience that you have had.

Date: _____

Dear _____ ,

Name _____ Date _____

Character Stamp

Title: _____ Author: _____

Important people are often recognized by an official postage stamp. The stamp shows a picture of the person or something they have accomplished.

1. **Choose a character from your text. Think about what you know about him or her. Then complete the chart below.**

CHARACTER	WHAT IS HE OR SHE LIKE?	WHAT DOES THIS CHARACTER LOVE?

2. **Use the information in your chart to design a stamp that shows the different qualities of the character.**

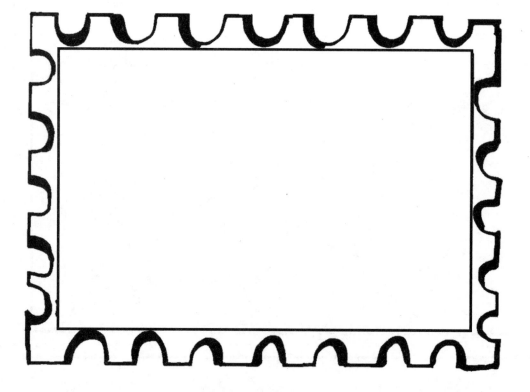

Name _____ Date _____

Character Playdate

Title: _____ Author: _____

Getting to know a character from a text is exciting. Readers can imagine what it would be like if they and the character were friends.

You have invited one of your favorite characters to your home. Which character in your book would you like to spend time with?

Character: _____

What would you like to do together? Think about everything you know about this character. Write about or draw pictures of the activities you want to do.

2 P.M.	3 P.M.	4 P.M.

Name _____ Date _____

My Opinion: Before, During, and After

Title: _____ Author: _____

Readers form opinions before, during, and after reading a text.

Answer these questions about your book.

BEFORE READING ⌐

Why did you choose to read this text?

DURING READING ⌐

Are you enjoying the text? Explain why or why not.

AFTER READING ⌐

Would you recommend this book to a friend? Explain why or why not.

Did your opinion of the text change as you read it? ☐ **YES** ☐ **NO**

If it did, explain how. _____

_____

_____

Name _____ Date _____

My Favorite Part

Choose a book that you have read.

Title: _____ Author: _____

Readers may decide that their favorite part of a story was particularly scary or funny. It's the part that they can easily remember.

Write about your favorite part of the book and explain why you liked it. Include details from the text.

_____
_____
_____
_____
_____
_____
_____
_____
_____
_____
_____
_____
_____
_____
_____
_____
_____
_____

Name _____ Date _____

What a Character

Title: _____ Author: _____

Readers form opinions about a character. They might think about how the character interacts with other characters or about whether the character reminds them of someone they know (including themselves).

Think about characters in your story and answer these questions.

Which character do you like best?

Why do you like this character? Support your answer with evidence from the story.

_____

_____

_____

_____

_____

_____

Name _____ Date _____

Book Advertisement

Choose a favorite book that you have read.

Title: _____ Author: _____

An advertisement tries to convince people to buy a product. Since advertisements are usually short, an author must choose his or her words carefully.

Write an advertisement for your book in the newspaper. Remember, you want to capture people's attention so they will want to buy and read the book. Share interesting details about the book, but don't give away everything—especially the ending!

Name _____ Date _____

Read This Book!

Title: _____ Author: _____

When readers really enjoy a text, they want to let others know about it. They may recommend a particular text to a friend because they know he or she likes a particular author or enjoys reading a particular genre, or because they usually like the same types of books.

Write a letter to a friend recommending your text. Tell your friend what you really liked about it and why you think he or she will enjoy it. Be persuasive so your friend will rush out and read the text!

Date: _____

Dear _____,

Name _____ Date _____

Author's Purpose

Title: _____ Author: _____

Authors write for several reasons. They may want to do one or more of the following:

★ *entertain*

★ *persuade readers to believe an idea*

★ *share information about a topic*

What do you think the author's main purpose was for writing this text? Circle one.

Entertain   Persuade   Inform

Why do you think so? Use evidence from the text to support your answer.

_____

_____

_____

_____

_____

_____

_____

_____

Visualize the Poem

Poem: _____ Poet: _____

Poets use language to evoke feelings, ideas, and images. They hope to inspire and awaken new feelings, ideas, and images in readers.

What image comes to mind when you read and think about your poem? Sketch it below. Then write about your drawing.

_____

_____

_____

_____

_____

_____

Name _____ Date _____

Poetic Response

Poem: _____ Poet: _____

The title of a poem can often give readers a clue as to what the poem will be about.

After reading the poem, answer the questions below.

What do you think of the poem's title?

What is the main idea of the poem? Support your answer with evidence from the poem.

If you could give this poem a different title, what would it be? Tell why you chose this title.

Language: Overview

We don't always give students enough opportunities to play with language and really demonstrate that they understand how the English language works. The activities in this section take the focus away from what is happening in a text and place it on authors' use of language to enhance their work. Students think about different types of sentences and how to punctuate them, recognize how dialogue can reveal much about characters in a text, and explore new vocabulary.

Activities:

Super Sentences: Students search for interesting sentences in their text and explain why they find them interesting.
> OBJECTIVE: *To identify new and interesting vocabulary and sentence structures*
> CCSS: RL/RI 3.1, 3.4, 3.10, 4.1, 4.4, 4.10, 5.1, 5.4, 5.10

More Super Sentences: Students search for interesting sentences in a text and explain what makes them interesting.
> OBJECTIVES: *To identify new and interesting vocabulary and sentence structures; to identify types of sentences*
> CCSS: RL/RI 3.1, 3.4, 3.10, 4.1, 4.4, 4.10, 5.1, 5.4, 5.10

Put the Point on It: Punctuation: Students focus on interesting sentences and different kinds of punctuation.
> OBJECTIVES: *To identify different types of sentences; to analyze the uses and purpose of punctuation*
> CCSS: RL/RI 3.1, 3.4, 3.10, 4.1, 4.4, 4.10, 5.1, 5.4, 5.10

Say It Like It Is: Dialogue: Students record and discuss dialogue to help them understand a character.
> OBJECTIVES: *To identify dialogue; to express an opinion*
> CCSS: RL 3.1, 3.4, 3.5, 3.10, 4.1, 4.4, 4.5, 4.10, 5.1, 5.4, 5.5, 5.10

Dialogue Sketch: Students record a dialogue between characters from a text, illustrate the accompanying interaction, and explain why this interaction is important to the story.
> OBJECTIVES: *To analyze dialogue between characters; to create an illustration of interactions between two characters from a text*
> CCSS: RL 3.3, 3.4, 3.10, 4.3, 4.4, 4.10, 5.3, 5.4, 5.10

Words of Wonder: Students focus on new vocabulary and use context clues to figure out the meaning of the words.
> OBJECTIVE: *To build vocabulary*
> CCSS: RL/RI 3.1, 3.4, 3.10, 4.1, 4.4, 4.10, 5.1, 5.4, 5.10

Picturing Vocabulary: Students show their understanding of interesting vocabulary by illustrating the meaning of the words.
> OBJECTIVES: *To deepen understanding of vocabulary; to use context clues; to visualize vocabulary*
> CCSS: RL/RI 3.4, 3.10, 4.4, 4.10, 5.4, 5.10

Vocabulary Web: Students complete a word web with the meaning of a word, synonyms, word associations, and antonyms.
> OBJECTIVES: *To deepen understanding of vocabulary words; to complete a word web; to identify denotative and connotative meanings; to identify synonyms and antonyms*
> CCSS: RL/RI 3.4, 3.10, 4.4, 4.10, 5.4, 5.10

Poetic Vocabulary: Students discuss words of their own choosing from a poem.
> OBJECTIVES: *To deepen understanding of vocabulary; to use context clues; to visualize vocabulary*
> CCSS: RL 3.4, 3.10, 4.4, 4.10, 5.4, 5.10

Name _____ Date _____

Super Sentences

Title: _____ Author: _____

Interesting sentences come in many shapes and sizes. An author uses vocabulary, punctuation, the rhythm of a sentence—and sometimes humor—to capture readers' attention.

Find "super sentences" in your reading that are interesting. Record them below. Tell why you like each sentence.

PAGE NUMBER	SENTENCES I LIKE	I LIKE THIS SENTENCE BECAUSE . . .

Name _____ Date _____

More Super Sentences

Title: _____ Author: _____

A sentence can be short and simple and still pack a punch. A compound or complex sentence can give readers more time to think more deeply about an idea.

Look for interesting sentences that make you stop and think. Write the sentence and name the type of sentence it is. Then tell why you like each sentence.

Sentence From Text:	Type of Sentence (*circle one*): Simple Compound Complex
Why I like this sentence:	

Sentence From Text:	Type of Sentence (*circle one*): Simple Compound Complex
Why I like this sentence:	

Sentence From Text:	Type of Sentence (*circle one*): Simple Compound Complex
Why I like this sentence:	

Put the Point on It: Punctuation

Title: _____ Author: _____

Look for an interesting sentence that captures your attention. Name the type of sentence it is. Think about how the author used punctuation in the sentence.

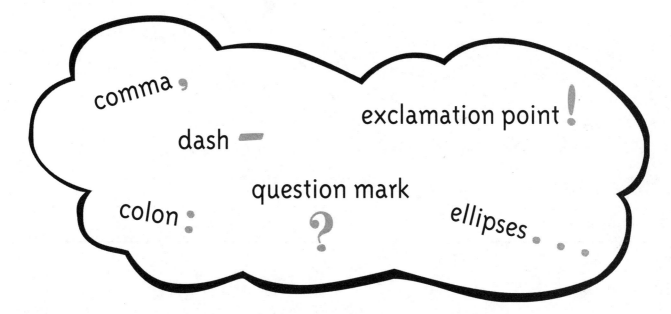

Sentence From Text:	Type of Sentence (*circle one*):
	Simple Compound Complex
Interesting Punctuation:	**Purpose of Punctuation:**

Name _____ Date _____

Say It Like It Is: Dialogue

Title: _____ Author: _____

Authors use dialogue to show how characters feel and think. Dialogue can help explain the following:

what one character thinks about another character

a new idea the character has

what a character hopes to accomplish

the feelings a character has

Write down dialogue that helps you understand a character in your book.

PAGE NUMBER	DIALOGUE	HOW THESE WORDS HELP ME UNDERSTAND THE CHARACTER

Name _____ Date _____

Dialogue Sketch

Title: _____ Author: _____

Dialogue is more than just two or more people talking to each other. Authors not only write the words that characters are saying, but they also describe their facial expressions and gestures to show how the characters are feeling.

Draw two characters from your book talking to each other.

EXAMPLE: If it is a happy conversation, the characters would be smiling. If it is an angry conversation, the characters might be raising their arms or their eyebrows might be pointing down.

Write the dialogue from your book to show how the characters are feeling. Use speech bubbles.

Why do you think this dialogue is important to the story?

_____

_____

_____

Name _____ Date _____

Words of Wonder

Title: _____ Author: _____

Readers often come across new words in a text. They don't always have a dictionary. They might think about a similar word that they know. They might look at smaller words within the word. They might look for clues in the sentence and in the sentence before and after it.

Record three unfamiliar or new words from your reading. Tell what you think each word means, based on how it is used in the text.

Word: _____

Sentence:

What I think the word means:

Word: _____

Sentence:

What I think the word means:

Word: _____

Sentence:

What I think the word means:

Name _____ Date _____

Picturing Vocabulary

Title: _____ Author: _____

It often helps readers to draw a picture of a new word to understand its meaning.

During your reading, choose three interesting words. Write the meaning of each word in your own words. Then tell what you visualize when you think of the word. For example, to show that you understand the word *elated*, you might describe a person celebrating or smiling from ear to ear.

Name _____ Date _____

Vocabulary Web

Title: _____ Author: _____

Synonyms are words that have similar meanings. Antonyms are words that have opposite meanings.

Write an unfamiliar or new word in the center of the word web. Include it in a sentence. Then complete the rest of the word web.

- Write the meaning of the word.
- Write two synonyms for the word.
- Think about the word. List five words that this word makes you think of.
- Write two antonyms for the word.

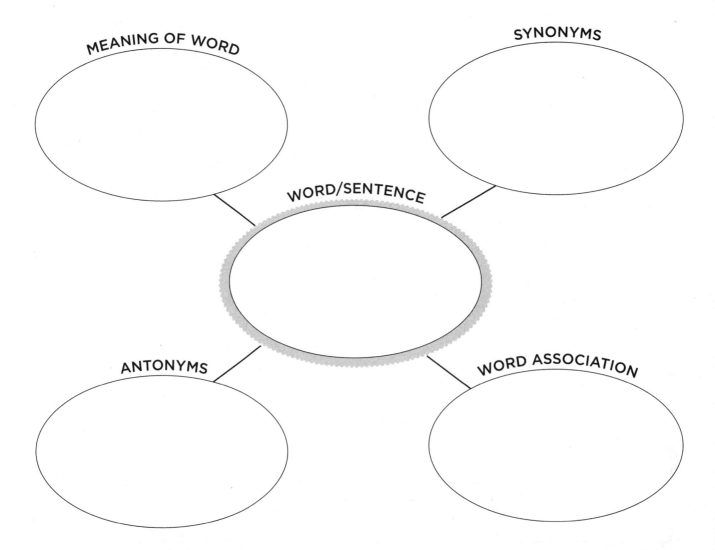

MEANING OF WORD

SYNONYMS

WORD/SENTENCE

ANTONYMS

WORD ASSOCIATION

Poetic Vocabulary

Poem: _____ **Poet:** _____

Words are fascinating. Readers notice interesting words; they may like the sound of a word, the images that come to mind when they read it, or its meaning.

Write down some words from the poem that you like.

Word: _____
Why I like the word:

Word: _____
Why I like the word:

Word: _____
Why I like the word:

Word: _____
Why I like the word:

References

Allington, R. L. (2012). *What really matters for struggling readers: Designing research-based programs* (3rd ed.). Boston: Pearson Education.

Hiebert, E. H., & Reutzel, D. R. (Eds.). (2010). *Revisiting silent reading: New directions for teachers and researchers.* Newark, DE: International Reading Association.

Patall, E. A., Cooper, H., & Wynn, S. R. (2010). The effectiveness and relative importance of choice in the classroom. *Journal of Educational Psychology, 102*(4), 896–915.

Professional Resources

Allington, R. L., & McGill-Franzen, A. (1993). What are they to read? Not all children, Mr. Riley, have easy access to books. *Education Week, 42*(10), 26.

Atwell, N. (2007). *The reading zone: How to help kids become skilled, passionate, habitual, critical readers.* New York: Scholastic.

Boyles, N. (2004). *Constructing meaning through kid-friendly comprehension strategy instruction.* Gainesville, FL: Maupin House.

Cullinan, B. E. (2000). *Independent reading and school achievement.* U.S. Department of Education. July 11, 2007, from www.ala.org/ala/aasl/aaslpubsandjournals/slmrb/slmrcontents/volume32000/ALA.

Ewing, R. (2006). *Beyond the reading wars: A balanced approach to helping children learn to read.* Newton, Australia: PETA.

Gotthelf, A., & Allyn, P. (2008). *The complete year in reading and writing: grade 3.* New York: Scholastic.

Harvey, S., & Goudvis, A. (2007). *Strategies that work: Teaching comprehension for understanding and engagement.* Portland, ME: Stenhouse.

Holliday, M. (2008). *Strategies for reading success.* Newton, Australia: PETA.

Hoyt, L., & Therriault, T. (2008). *Mastering the mechanics: Ready-to-use lessons for modeled, guided, and independent editing, grades 2–3 and grades 4–5.* New York: Scholastic.

Marshall, J. C. (2002). *Are they really reading? Expanding SSR in the middle grades.* Portland, ME: Stenhouse.

Pastore, L., & Allyn, P. (2008). *The complete year in reading and writing, grade 4.* New York: Scholastic.

Pastore, L., & Allyn, P. (2008). *The complete year in reading and writing, grade 5.* New York: Scholastic.

Rossbridge, J., & Rushton, K. (2010). *Conversations about text: Teaching grammar using literary texts.* Newton, Australia: PETA.

Samuels, S. J. (2006). Toward a model of reading fluency. In S. J. Samuels & A. E. Fastrup (Eds.), *What research has to say about fluency instruction* (pp. 24–46). Newark, DE: International Reading Association.

Sibberson, F., & Szymusiak, K. (2003). *Still learning to read: Teaching students in grades 3–6.* Portland, ME: Stenhouse.

Vitale-Reilly, P., & Allyn, P. (2008). *The complete year in reading and writing, grade 2.* New York: Scholastic.

Appendix: Leveled-Book Suggestions

This list represents a very small sampling of great books we love. There are so many, many more. The key for independent reading is to be sure that your students are involved in selection and in learning how to make their own choices and that the independent reading helps them build stamina, fluency, comprehension and decoding skills. Beyond this, the selections they make should help them fortify and deepen their own lifelong reading lives.

LEVEL 24

AUTHOR	TITLE
Selby B. Beeler	*Throw Your Tooth on the Roof: Tooth Traditions Around the World*
Jeff Brown	*Flat Stanley*
Anthony Browne	*The Shape Game*
	Zoo
Eve Bunting	*The Wednesday Surprise*
J. Cotton	*Veteran's Day*
Tomie dePaola	*Strega Nona*
Kate DiCamillo	Mercy Watson series
Gail Gibbons	*My Baseball Book*
Stephen Krensky	*Christopher Columbus*
Eva Moore	*The Truth About Bats*
Mary Pope Osbourne	*Rain Forests: A Nonfiction Companion to Afternoon on the Amazon*
Patricia Polacco	*Mr. Lincoln's Way*
Cynthia Rylant	High Rise Private Eyes eries
Marjorie Weinman	Nate the Great series
Various authors	Magic School Bus Science Chapter Book series
Vera Williams	*A Chair for My Mother*
Jane Yolen	Commander Toad series

LEVEL 28

AUTHOR	TITLE
Tony Abbott	Secrets of Droon series
Marc Brown	Arthur series
Eve Bunting	*Fly Away Home*
Eloise Greenfield	*Honey, I Love and Other Love Poems*
Dan Gutman	My Weird School series
Mike Kennedy	Soccer and other A True Book Scholastic series
Megan McDonald	Judy Moody series
	Stink series
Anna Pavlova	*I Dreamed I Was a Ballerina*
Mary Pope Osbourne	*Christmas in Camelot*
	Night of the New Magicians
	Winter of the Ice Wizard
Patricia Polacco	*When Lightning Comes in a Jar*
	The Bee Tree
	My Rotten Redheaded Older Brother
	John Phillip Duck

AUTHOR	TITLE
Patricia Polacco	*Thundercake*
Cynthia Rylant	*Thimbleberry stories*
	Mr Griggs' Work
	Lighthouse Family series
	Cobble Street Cousins series
Andrew Santella	*Jackie Robinson Breaks the Color Line*
Scholastic	Face-to-Face series
Barbara Taylor	*Sharks*
World Discovery History Readers	*North American Explorers*

LEVEL 30

AUTHOR	TITLE
Annie Barrows	Ivy and Bean series
Gilda Berger	*Do Whales Have Belly Buttons?*
Clyde Robert Bulla	*The Chalkbox Kid*
Eve Bunting	*Dreaming of America: An Ellis Island Story*
	Dandelions
	The Wall
Ann Cameron	*The Stories Julian Tells*
Elizabeth Dami	Geronimo Stilton series
Carmen Agra Deedy	*14 Cows for America*
Ruth Stiles Gannett	*My Father's Dragon*
James Cross Giblin	*George Washington: A Picture Book Biography*
Arnold Lobel	*Fables*
Steven Kellogg	*Pecos Bill: A Tall Tale*
Eva Moore	*Wild Whale Watch*
Mary Pope Osbourne	*Mummies in the Morning*
	Night of the New Magicians
	Pilgrims: A Nonfiction Companion to Thanksgiving on Thursday
Patricia Polacco	*Chicken Sunday*
Peter Roop	*Take a Giant Leap, Neil Armstrong!*
Ron Roy	A to Z Mysteries series
Jane Yolen	*Encounter*

LEVEL 34

AUTHOR	TITLE
Tony Abbott	Secrets of Droon series
Jean Betancourt	*Ten True Animal Rescues*
Jeff Brown	Flat Stanley series
Beverly Cleary	*Henry Huggins*

Beverly Cleary	*Runaway Ralph*
	Socks
	The Mouse and the Motorcycle
	Ramona and Beezus
Gail Gibbons	*Penguins*
	Polar Bears
	Star Gazers
	Grizzly Bears
Nikki Grimes	*Dyamonde Daniel series*
Suzy Kline	*Herbie Jones series*
Eva Moore	*Magic School Bus Science Chapter Books series*
James Stevenson	*Just Around the Corner: Poems*
R. L. Stine	*Goosebumps series*
Jane Yolen	*Owl Moon*

LEVEL 38

AUTHOR	TITLE
Derrick Barnes	*Ruby and The Booker Boys series*
Gilda & Melvin Berger .	*Where Have All The Pandas Gone?*
James Buckley, Jr.	*NBA Superstars*
Eve Bunting	*Smoky Night*
Tomie dePaola	*The Legend of the Bluebonnet*
John R. Erickson	Hank The Cowdog series
James Cross Giblin . . .	*Fireworks, Picnics and Flags: The Story of the Fourth of July*
Dick King-Smith	*The School Mouse*
	The Invisible Dog
	George Speaks
	Lady Lollipop/Clever Lollipop
Lois Lowry	*Gooney Bird Greene*
Christopher Maynard . .	*Days of the Knights: A Tale of Castles and Battles*
Ken Mochizuki	*Baseball Saved Us*
Jack Prelutsky	*The Beauty of the Beast: Poems From the Animal Kingdom*
Louis Sachar	Wayside School series
James Stevenson	*Popcorn: Poems*
Valerie Worth	*Peacock and Other Poems*
Malcolm Yorke	*Beastly Tales: Yeti, Big Foot, and the Loch Ness Monster*

LEVEL 40

AUTHOR	TITLE
Avi	*The Secret School*
Michael Buckley	Sisters Grimm series
James Buckley, Jr.	*NBA Reader: All-Time Super Scorers*
Eve Bunting	*Gleam and Glow*
Betsy Byars, Laurie . . . Myers, Betsy Duffey	*The SOS File*
Andrew Clements	*Frindle*
Roald Dahl	*The Twits*
Sid Fleischman	*The Whipping Boy*
Nikki Grimes	*A Dime a Dozen*
Dan Gutman	*Satch and Me*

Daisy Kerr	*Ancient Greeks*
Dick King-Smith	*Funny Frank*
	Pigs Might Fly
Lois Lowry	*Gooney Bird Greene and the Room Mother*
Patricia MacLachlan . .	*Sarah, Plain and Tall*
Mary Packard	*World's Weirdest Critters*
Thomas Rockwell	*How to Eat Fried Worms*
Seymour Simon	*Horses*
Judith St. George	*So You Want to Be President?*
Sarah L. Thomson	*Where Do Polar Bears Live?*
Susan Truesdell	*Hey World, Here I Am!*
Marcia K. Vaughan	*Up the Learning Tree*

LEVEL 44

AUTHOR	TITLE
Michael Burgan	*The Story of Levi's*
Ilene Cooper	*Sam I Am*
Bernard Evslin	*Heroes and Monsters of Greek Myth*
Charlotte Foltz Jones . .	*Mistakes That Worked: 40 Familiar Inventions and How They Came to Be*
Cornelia Funke	Ink Trilogy books
Beatrice Gormley	*First Ladies: Women Who Called the White House Home*
Sarah Weeks	*So B It: A Novel*
Dick King-Smith	*The Nine Lives of Aristotle*
C. S. Lewis	Chronicles of Narnia books
Beverley Naidoo	*Out of Bounds: Seven Stories of Conflict and Hope*
Seymour Simon	*Earthquakes*
	The Universe
Lemony Snicket	Series of Unfortunate Events books
Jacquelin Woodson . .	*Locomotion*
Laurence Yep	*The Rainbow People*

LEVEL 50

AUTHOR	TITLE
Melvin Berger	*Think Factory: Amazing Inventions*
Christopher Paul Curtis .	*Bud, Not Buddy*
Roald Dahl	*The BFG*
	Boy: Tales of Childhood
Gail Gibbons	*Galaxies, Galaxies!*
John Hareas	*LeBron James*
Susie Hodge	*Claude Monet*
Robert Lawson	*Ben and Me: An Astonishing Life of Benjamin Franklin by His Good Mouse Amos*
Kadir Nelson	*We Are the Ship: The Story of Negro League Baseball*
Katherine Patterson . .	*Bridge to Terabithia*
Patricia Polacco	*Pink and Say*
Cynthia Rylant	*A Blue-Eyed Daisy*
Barbara Rogasky	*Winter Poems*
Louis Sachar	*Holes*
Seymour Simon	*Volcanoes*
Jerry Spinelli	*Wringer*
	Loser
	Crash